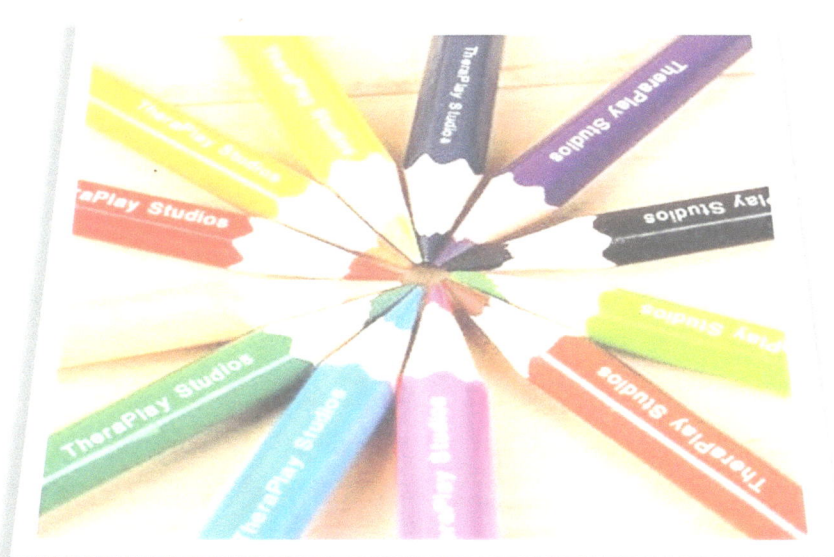

Copyright © 2019 by Diana Ezell /Art Theraplaystudios Color Therapy

All rights reserved. No part of this book may be reproduced or transmitted in any form or by any means without written permission from the author.

Thera~Play

Color Therapy Book

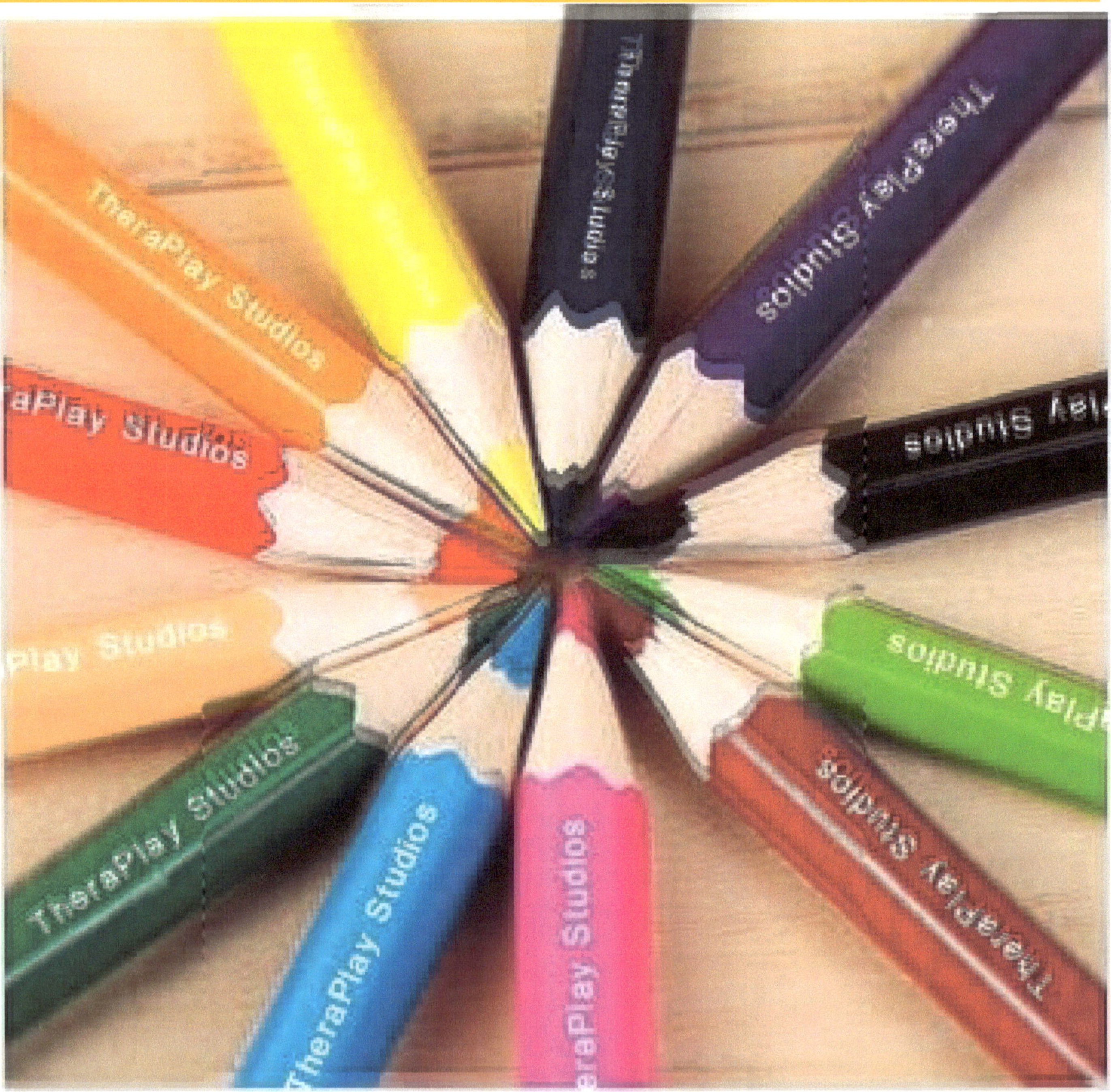

About

Art Thera~Play Studios is created by Diana Ezell as an outlet that is healing and helpful for all ages to combine playing with art. She has a Masters of Science in Human Services; specialized in Mental health counseling; Play Therapy Certificate from Capella University; and a Bachelors of Arts in Psychology from Ashford University. She enjoys feeding off the techniques of Art Therapy a form of expressive therapy that uses the creative process of making art to improve a person's physical, mental, and emotional well-being.

Thera~Play is here to encourage creative healing and entertainment. People think of therapy as a cookie cut sit on the couch and talk to a therapist. However here at Art Thera~Play Studios we want to get you engaged in your healing process of daily struggles; from mental health illnesses, grief, anxiety, stress and more. The creative process involved in expressing one's self artistically can help people to resolve issues as well as develop and manage their behaviors and feelings, reduce stress, and improve self-esteem and awareness.

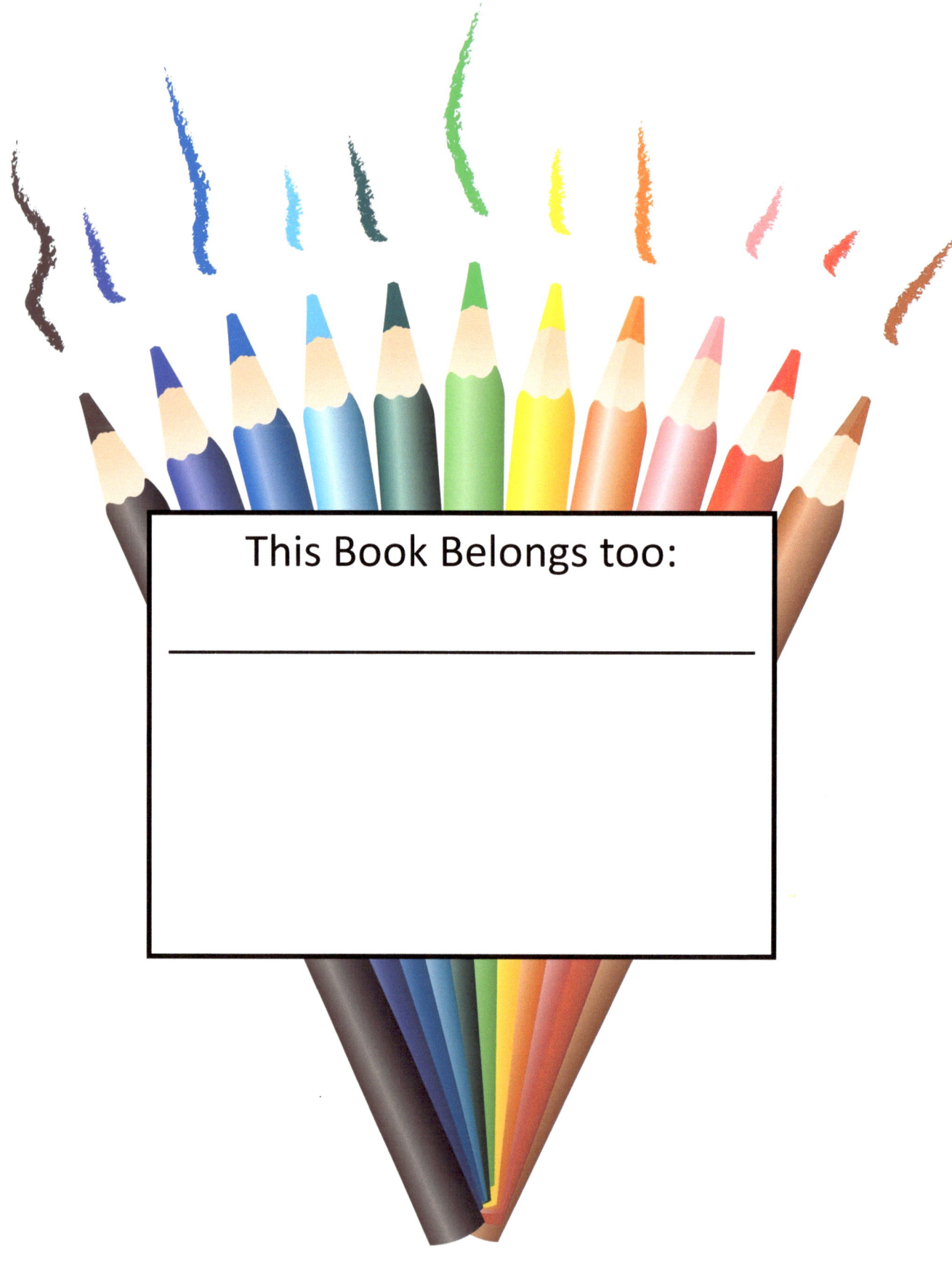

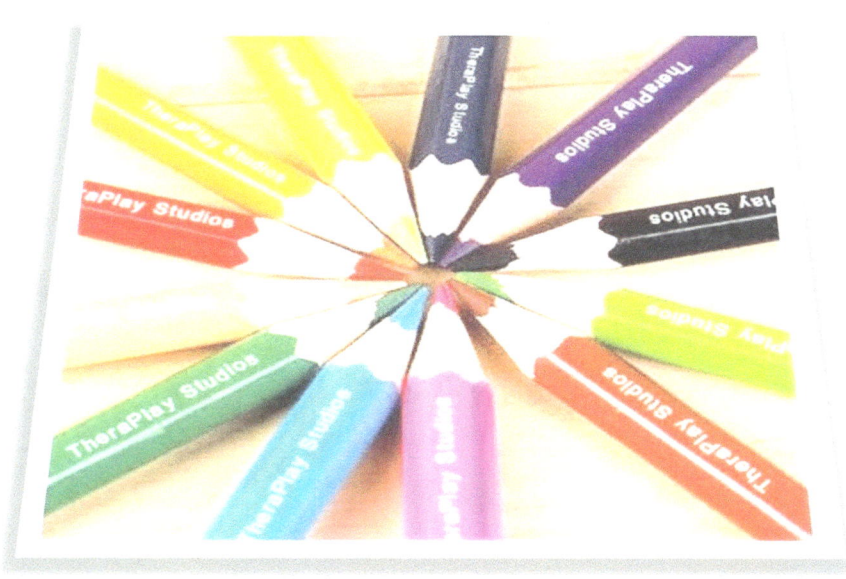

Color Meanings

blue	red	black	green
TRUST	LOVE	BOLD	SOOTHING
SMART	IMMEDIACY	RICH	ECO-FREINDLY
CALM	ENERGY	POWER	NATURAL
FAITH	SALE	MYSTERY	ENVY
NATURAL	PASSION	ELEGANCE	JEALOUSY
STABLE	ANGER	EVIL	BALANCE
POWER	HUNGER	STRENGTH	RESTFUL

yellow	orange	pink	purple
CHEER	HEALTH	TENDERNESS	ROYAL
ATTENTION	ATTRACTION	SENSITIVE	MYSTERIOUS
CHILDISH	STAND OUT	CARING	ARROGANT
FRESH	THIRST	EMOTIONAL	LUXURY
WARMTH	WEALTH	SYMPATHETIC	CHILDISH
ENERGY	YOUTHFUL	LOVE	CREATIVE
OPTIMISM	HAPPINESS	SEXUALITY	SADNESS

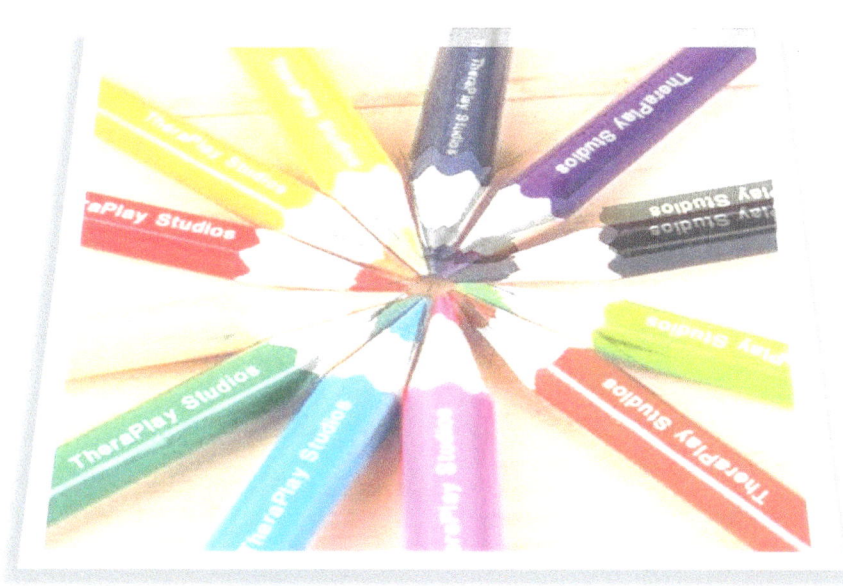

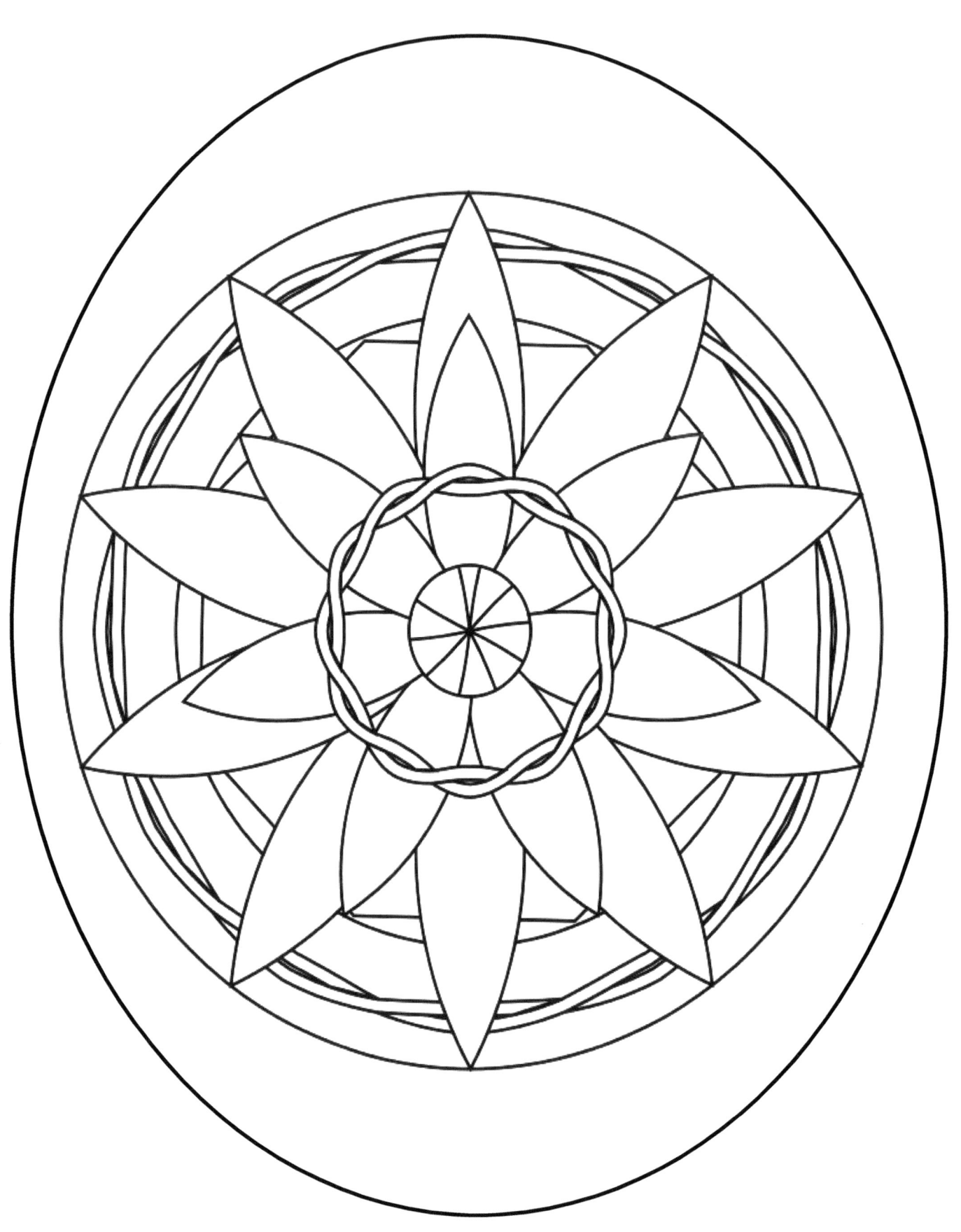

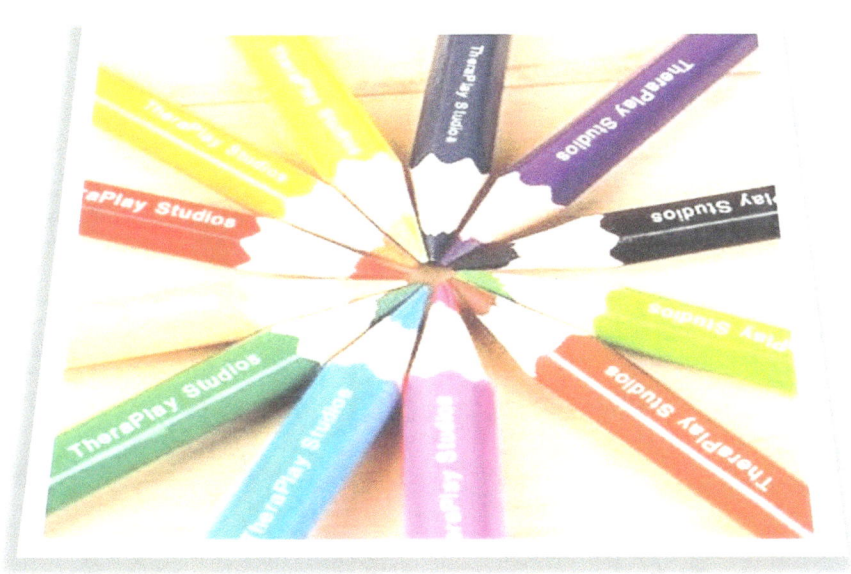

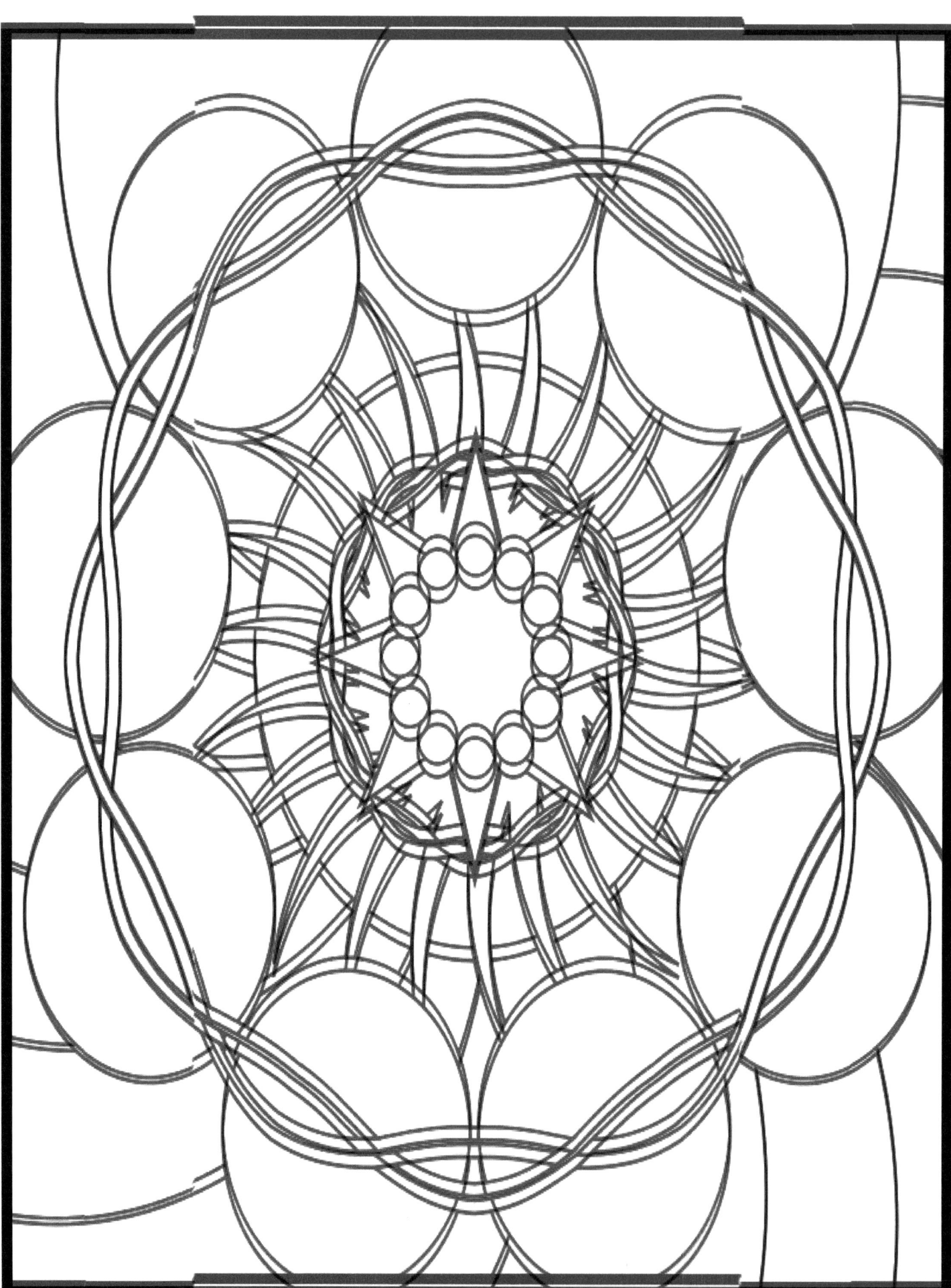

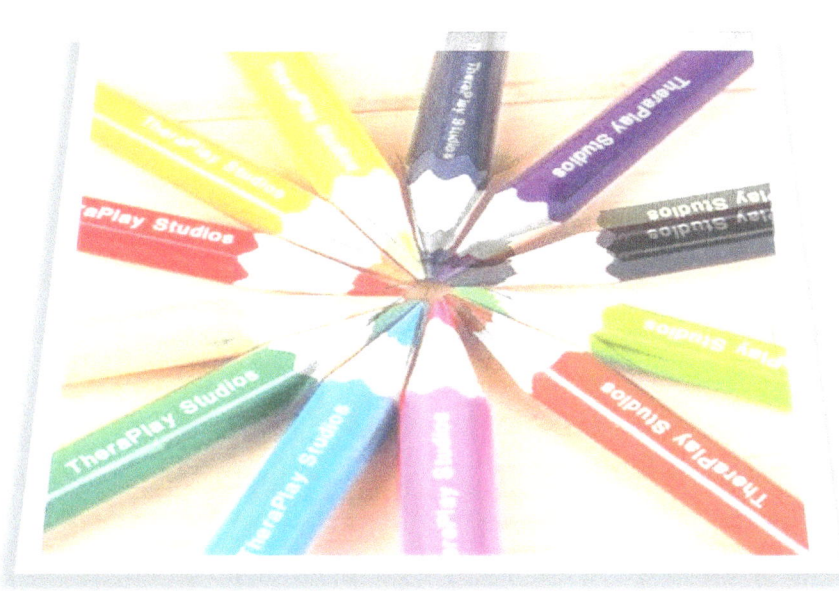

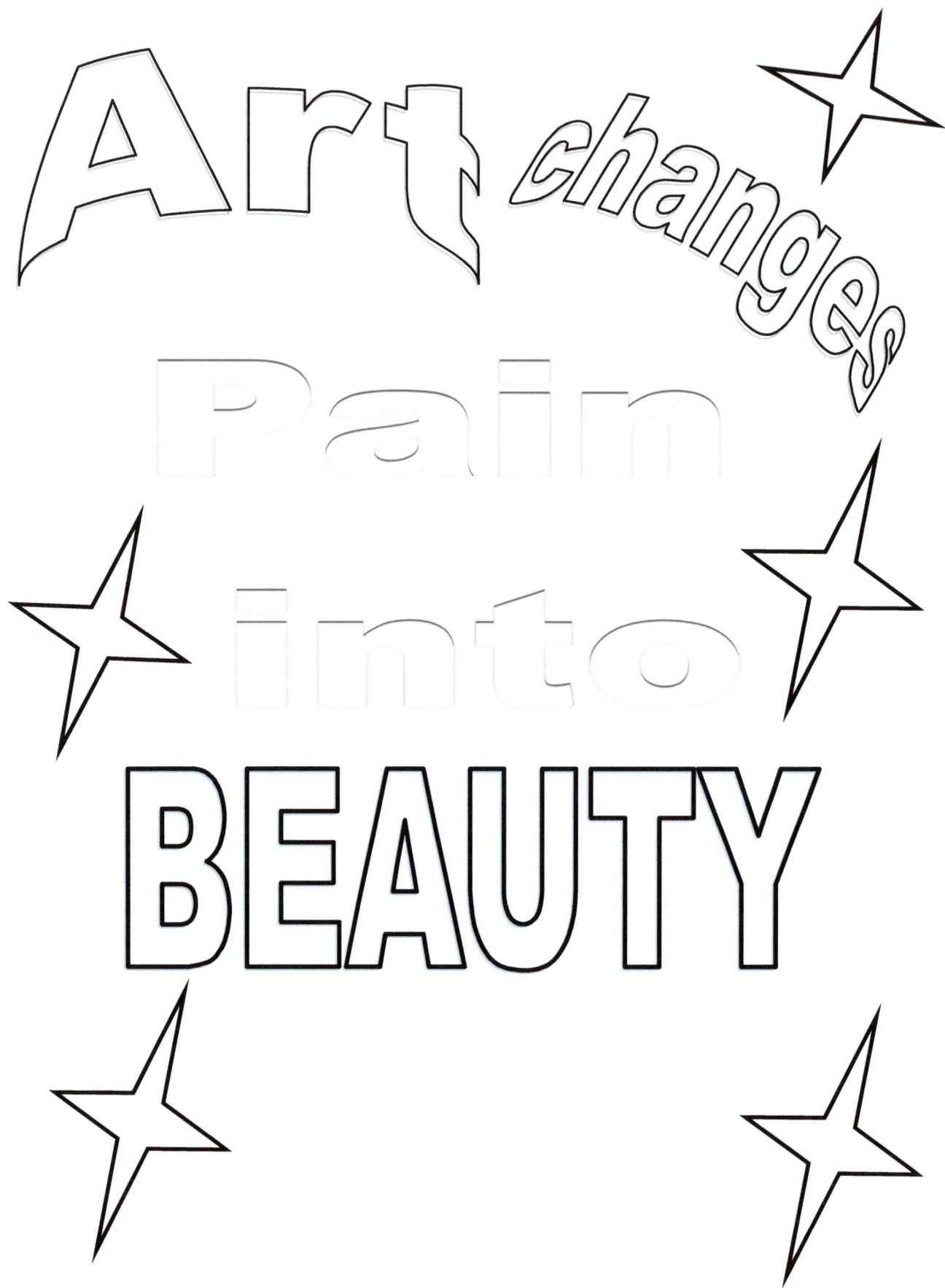

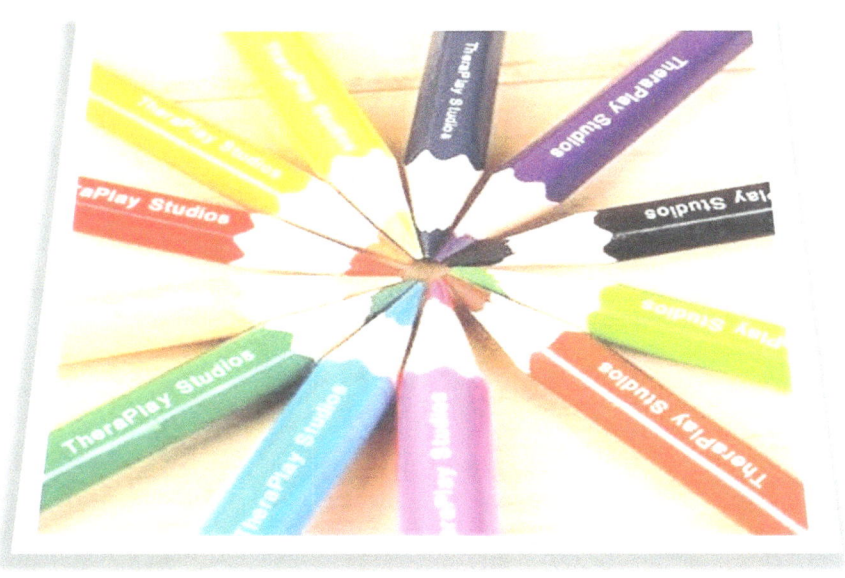

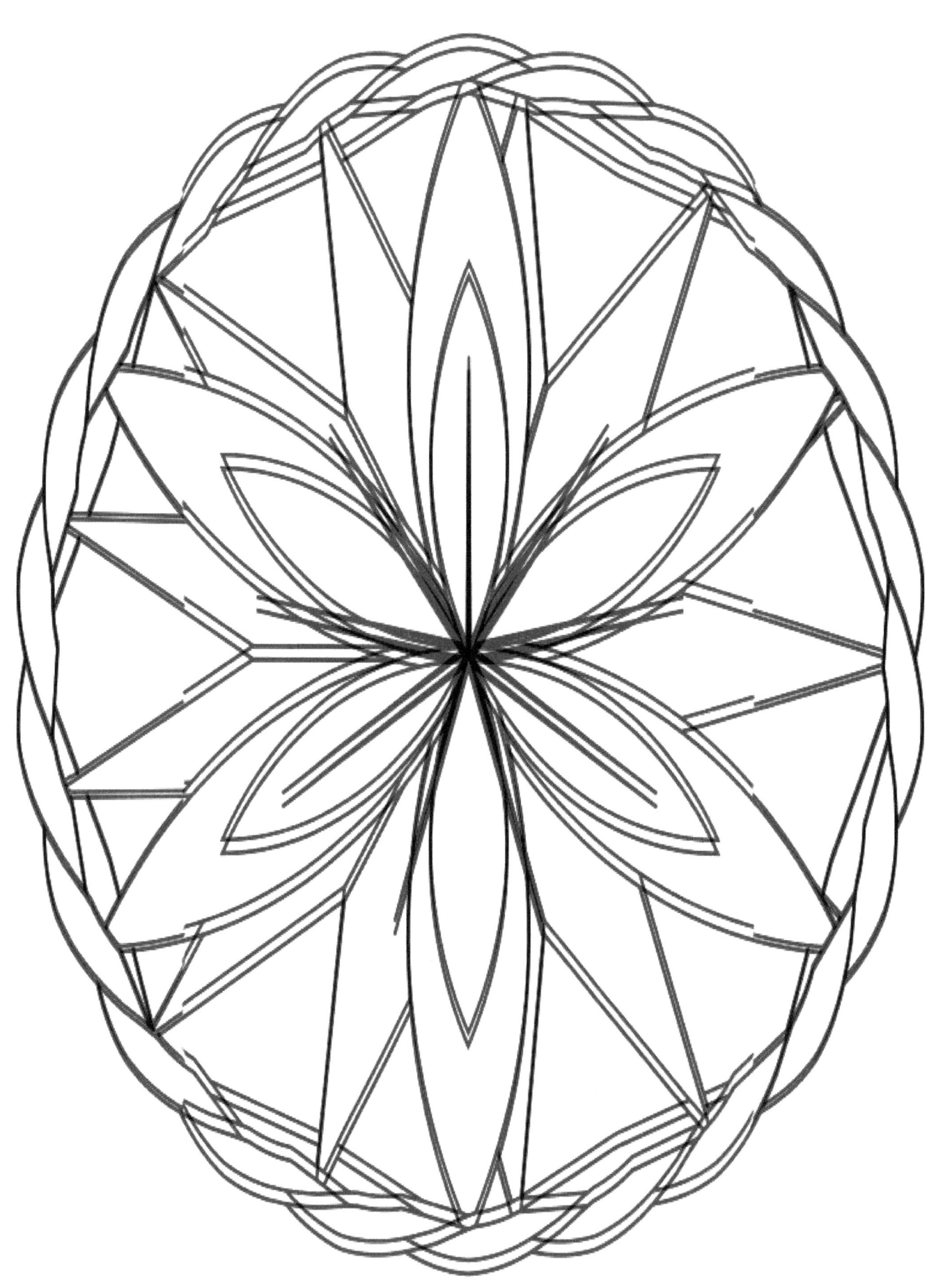

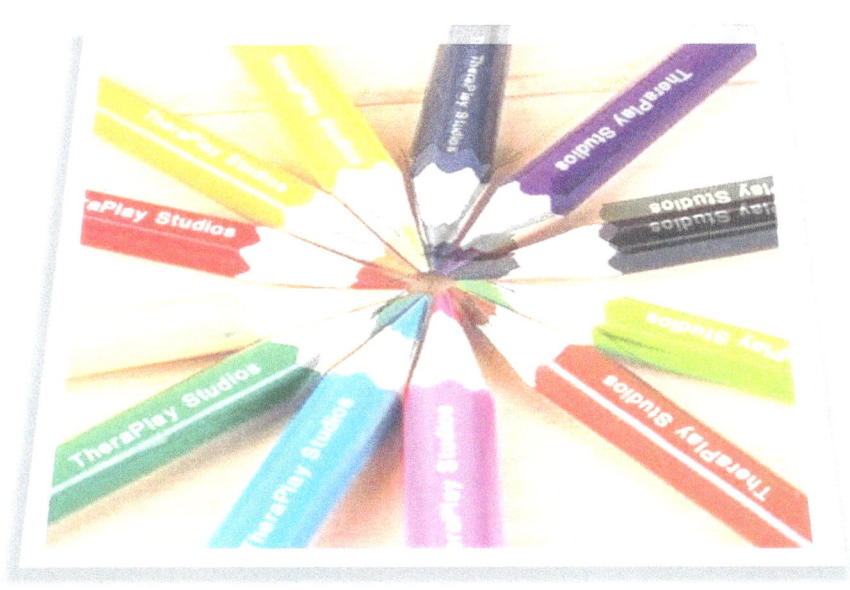

THE EMOTIONS OF COLOR

Reds
EXCITEMENT
PASSION
DANGER

Blues
TRUST
RELIABILITY
COOLNESS

Yellows
WARMTH
CHEER
HAPPINESS

Oranges
PLAYFULNESS
WARMTH
VIBRANCE

Greens
NATURE
FRESHNESS
GROWTH

Purples
ROYALTY
SPIRITUALITY
DIGNITY

Pastels
SOFTNESS
NURTURE
SECURITY

Whites
PURENESS
CLEAN
YOUTHFUL

Blacks
SOPHISTICATED
ELEGANT
MYSTERY

Golds
PRESTIGE
EXPENSIVE
ELEGANT

Silvers
PRESTIGE
COLD
SCIENTIFIC

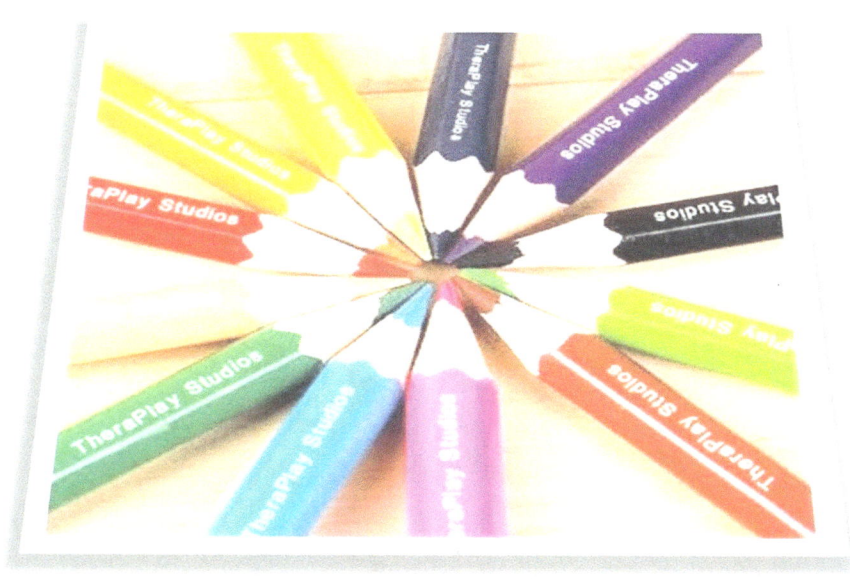

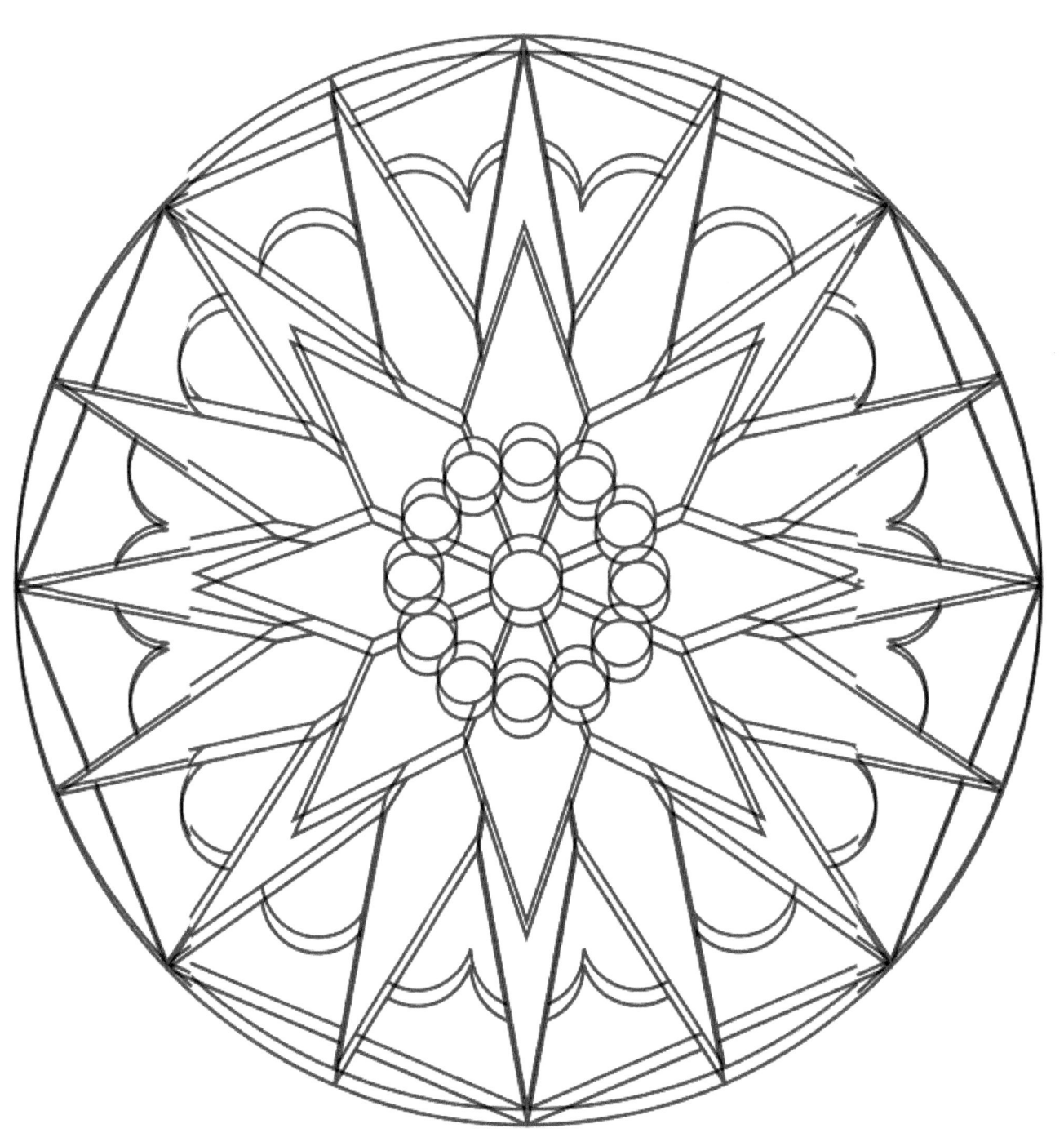

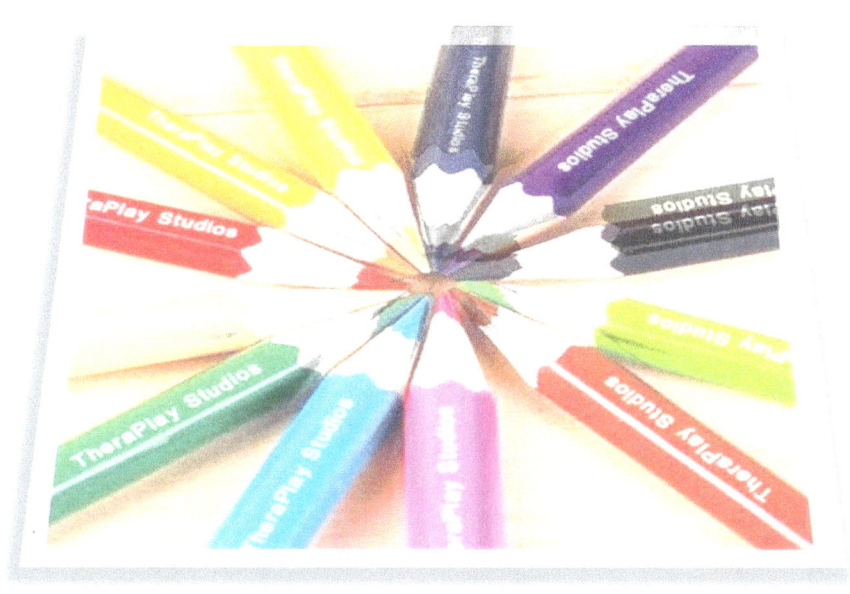

I ♥ Art Therapy

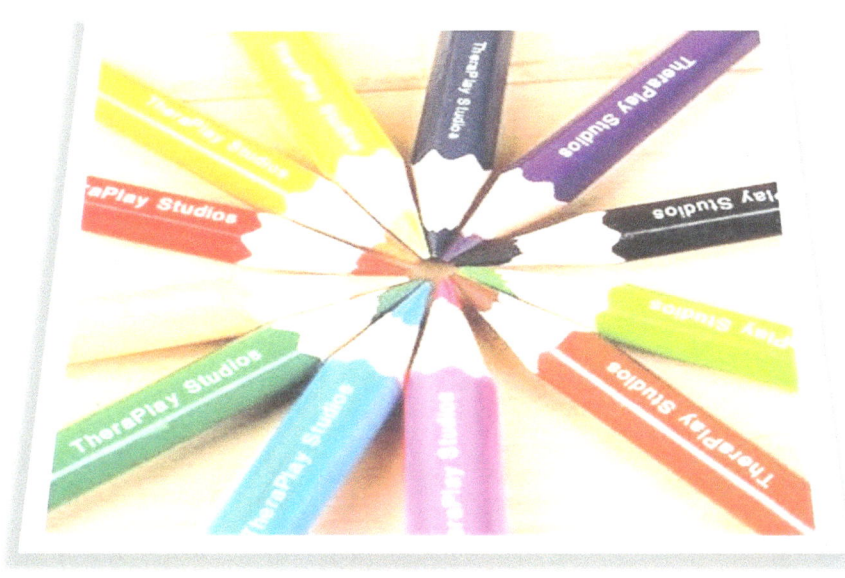

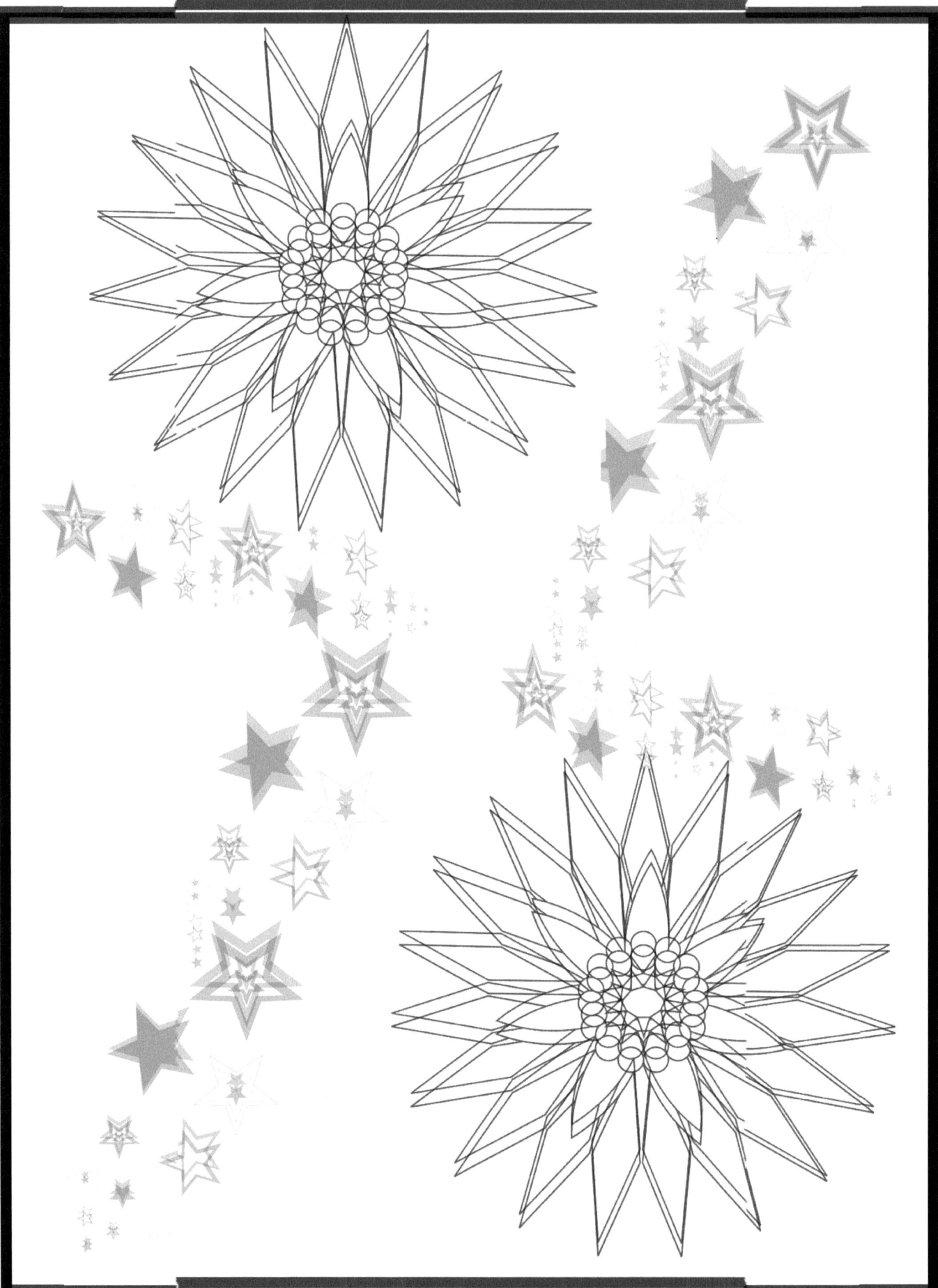

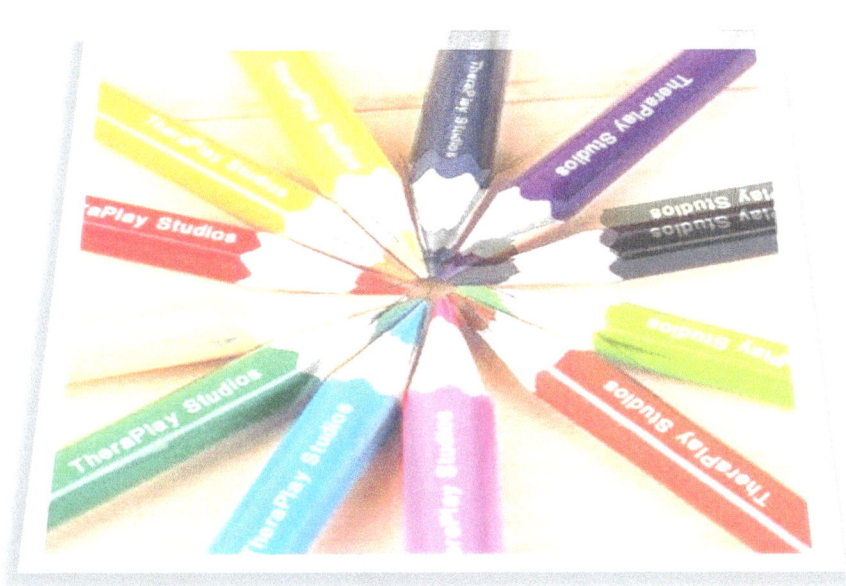

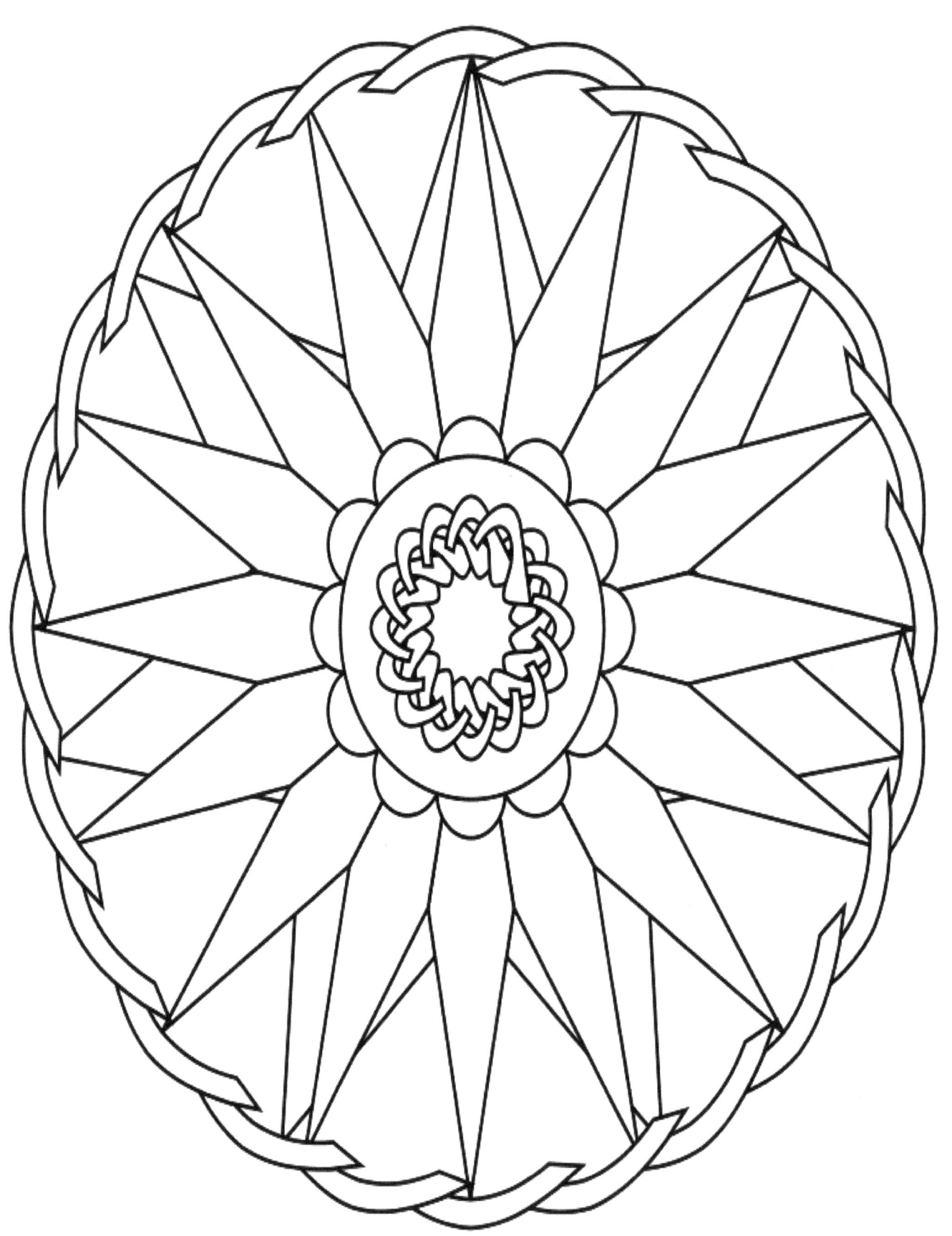

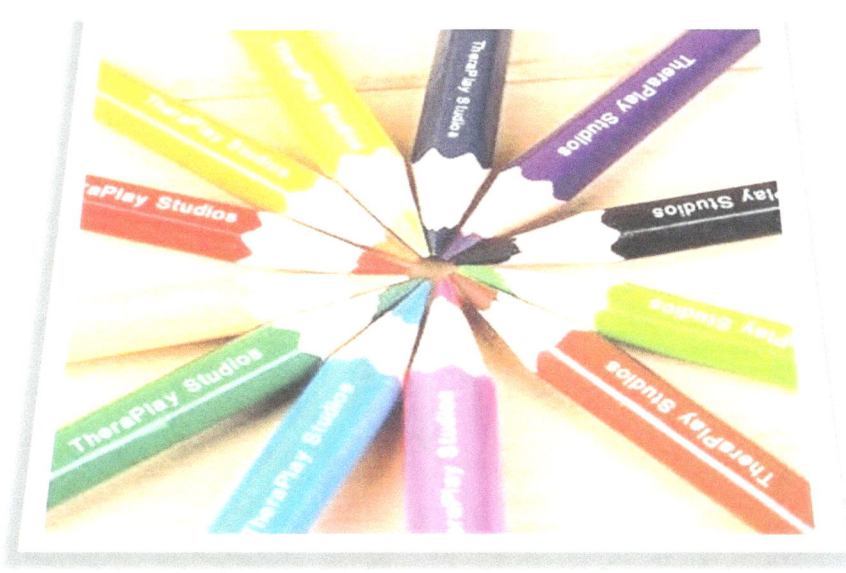

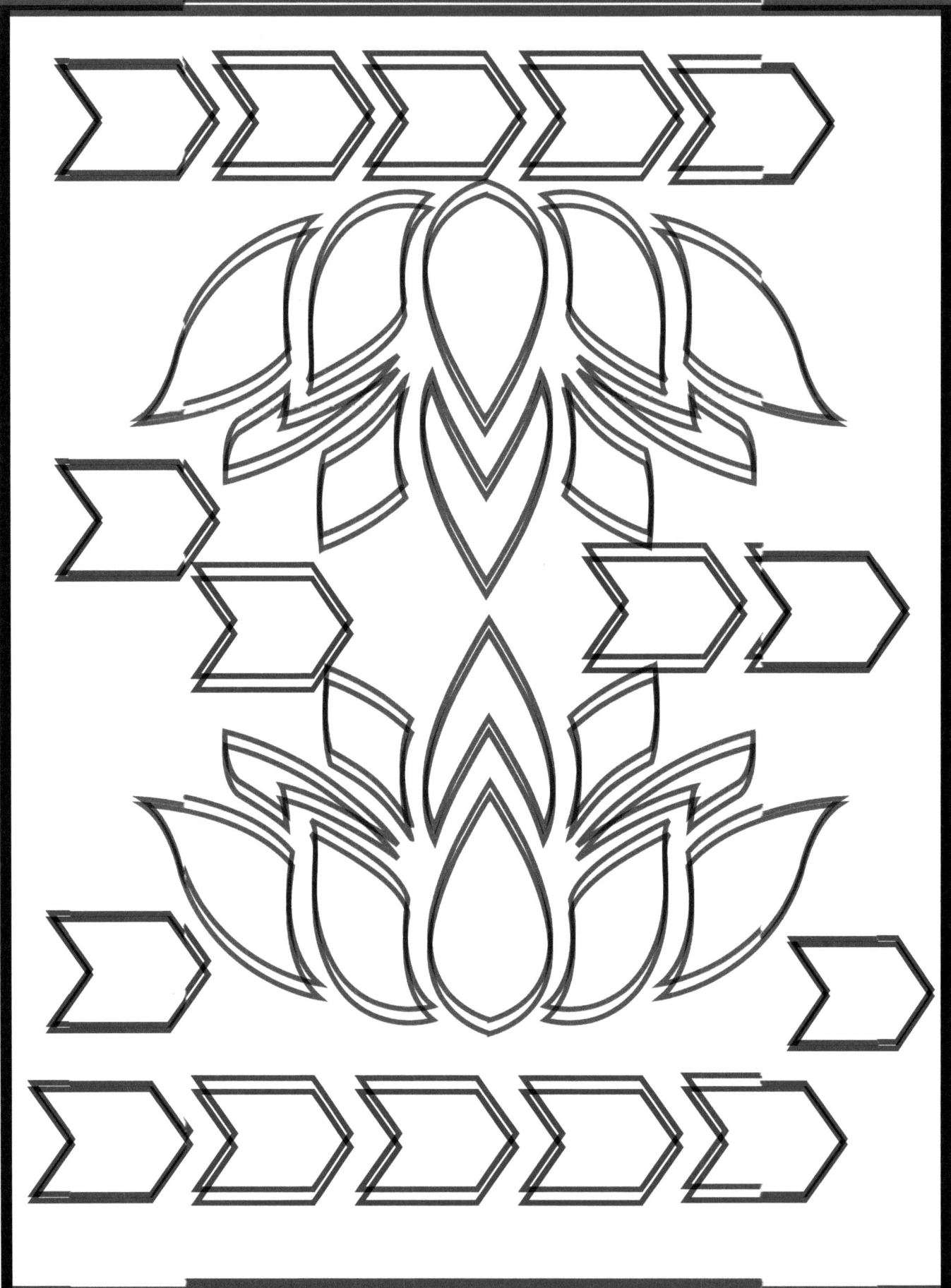

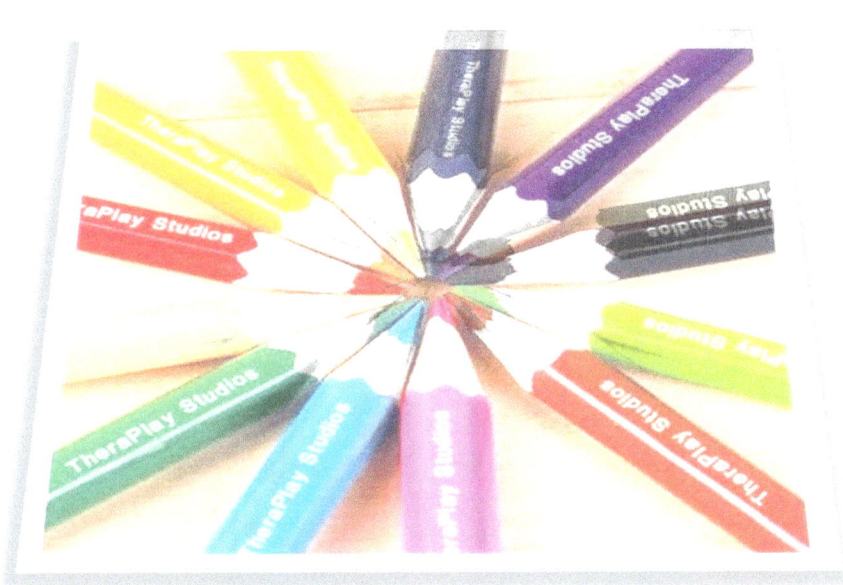

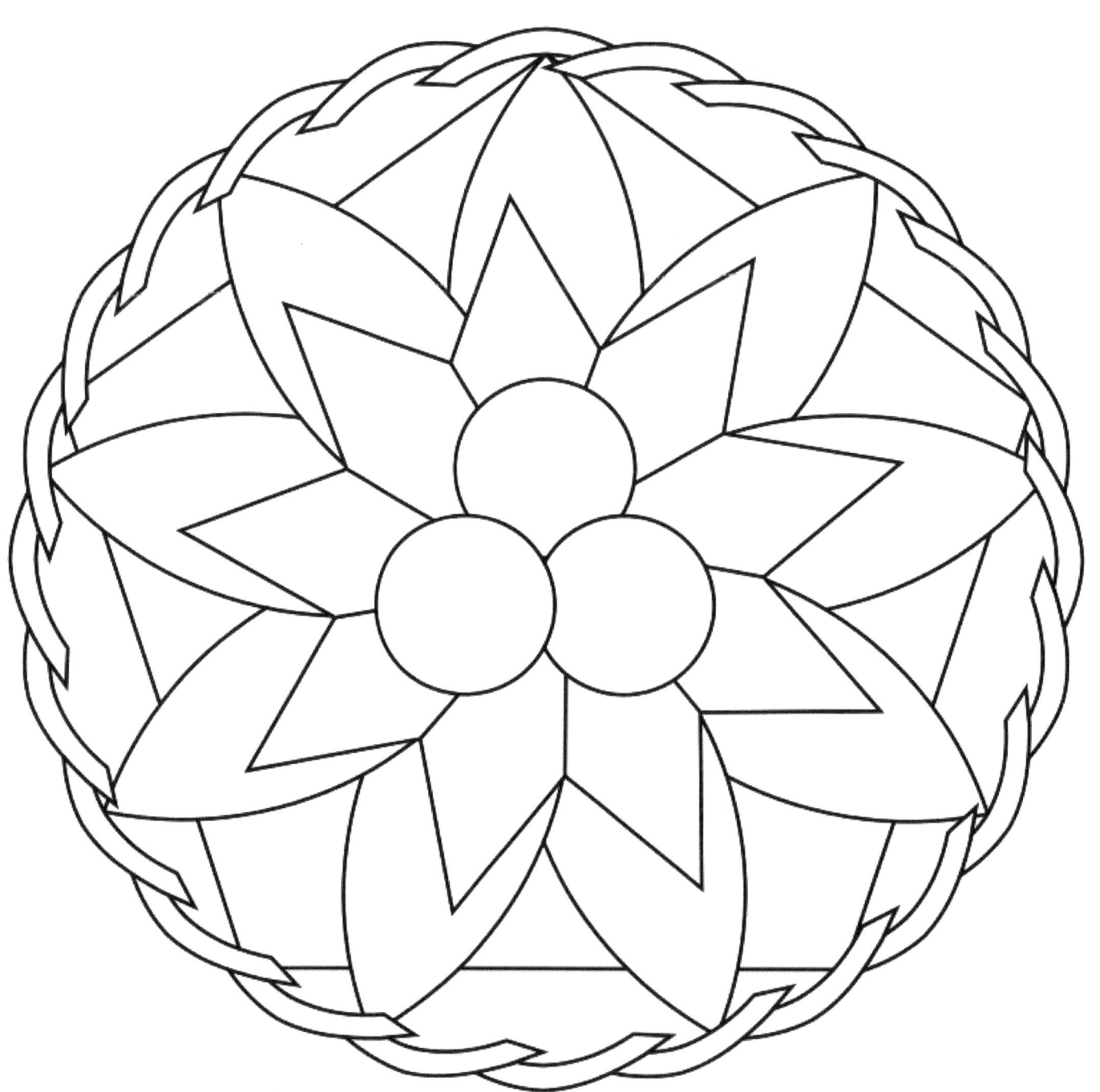

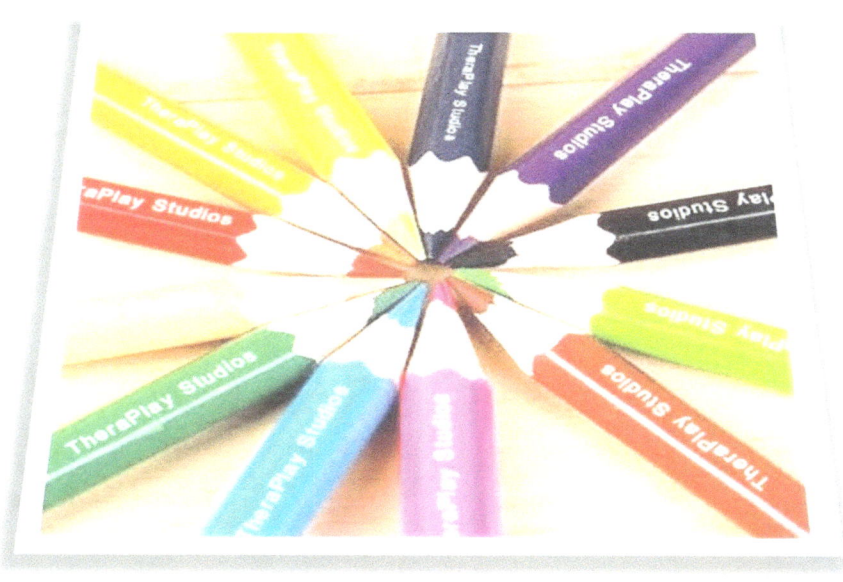

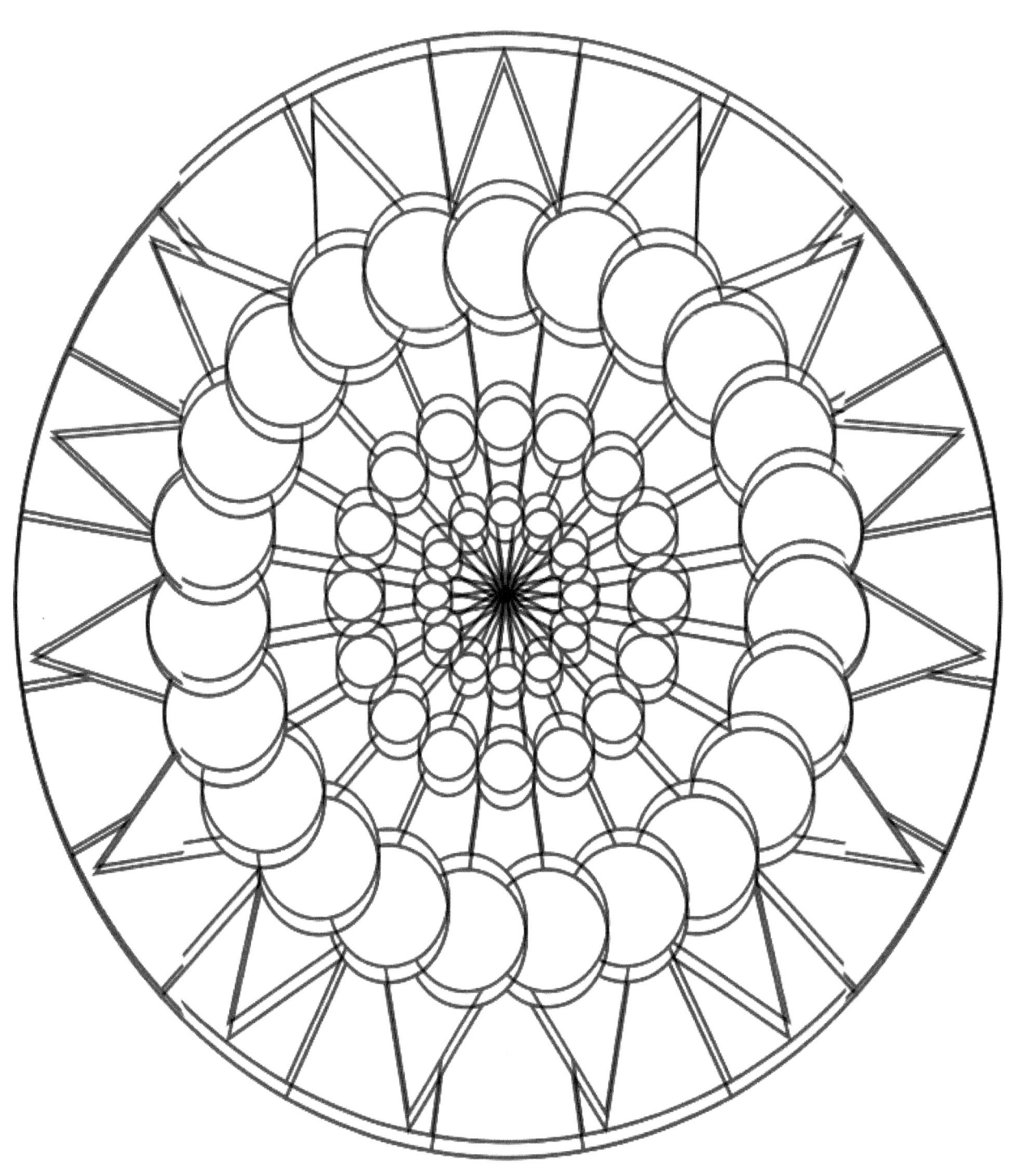

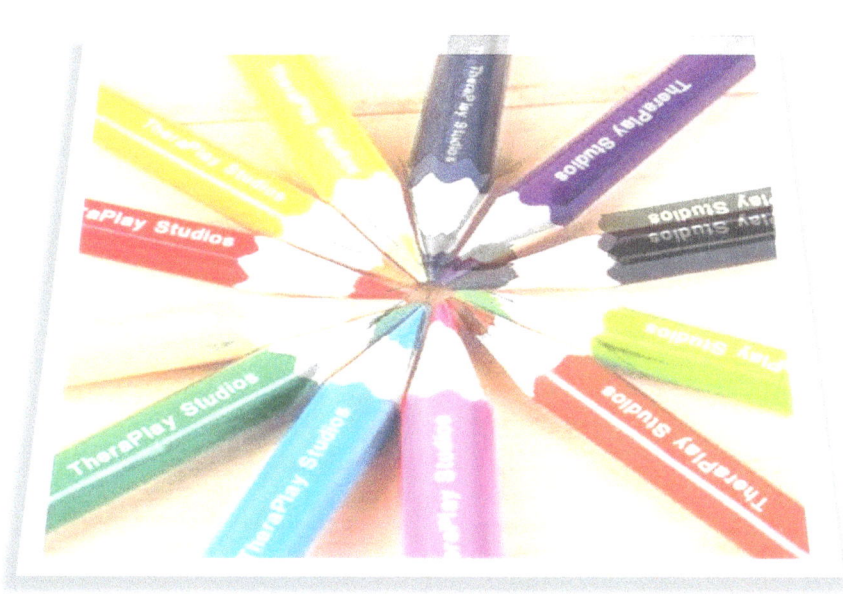

Make your own color wheel

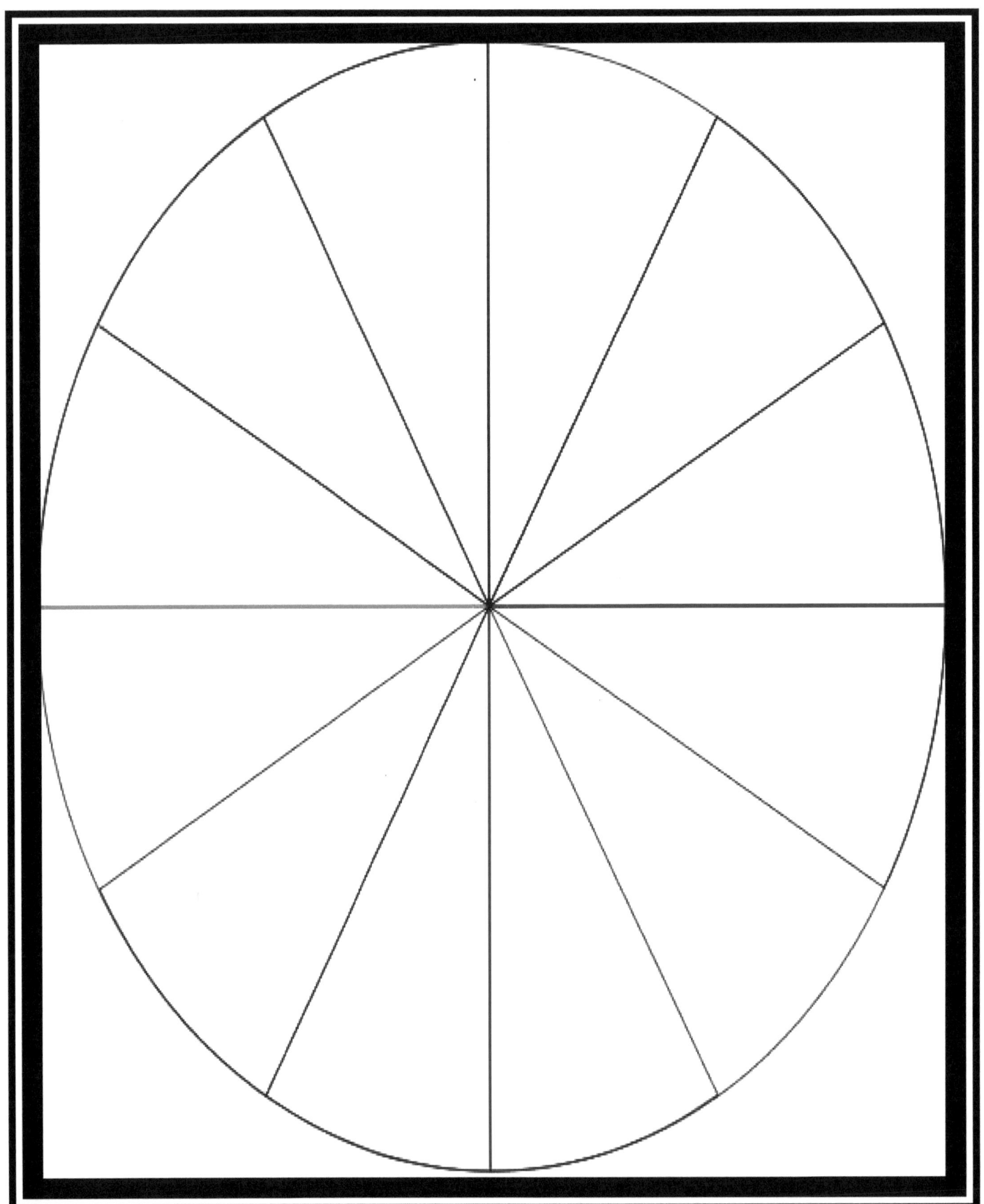

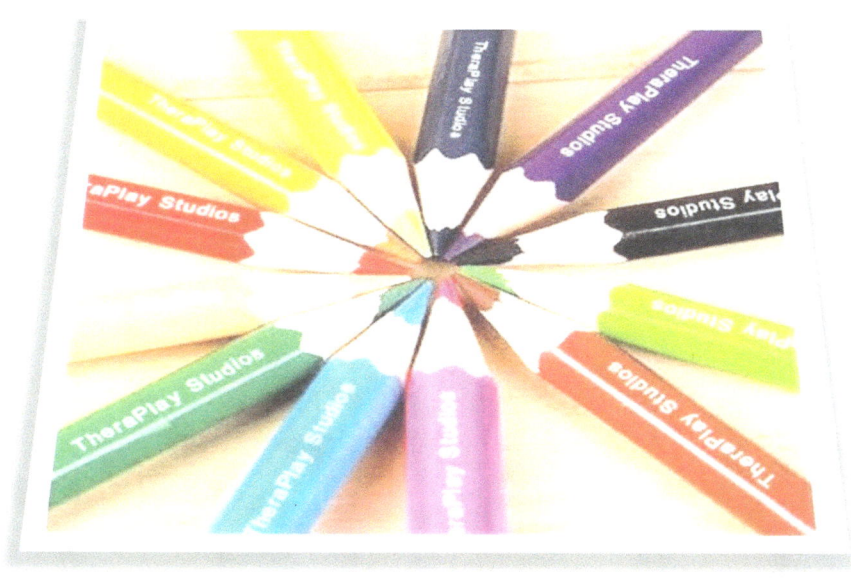

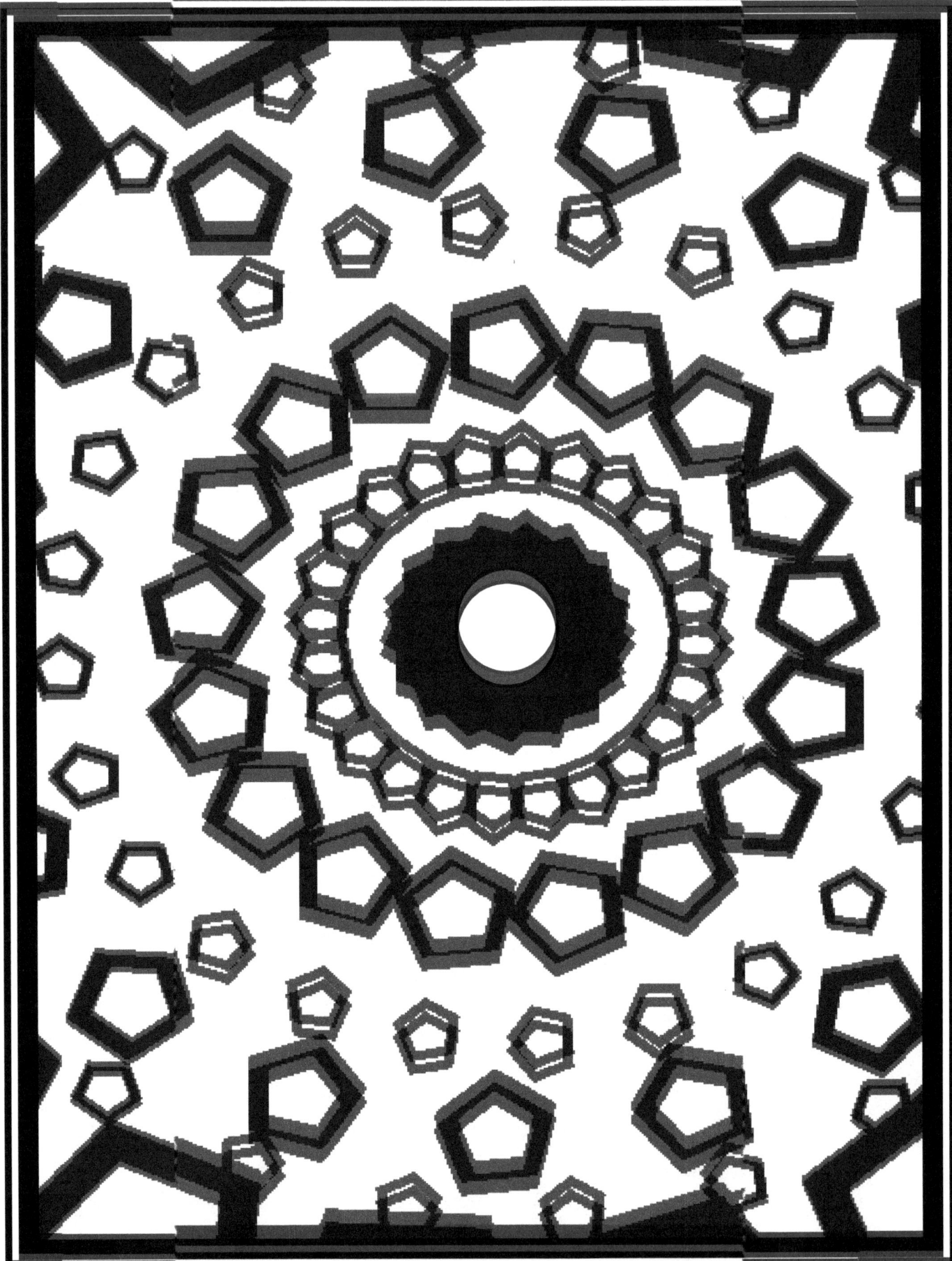

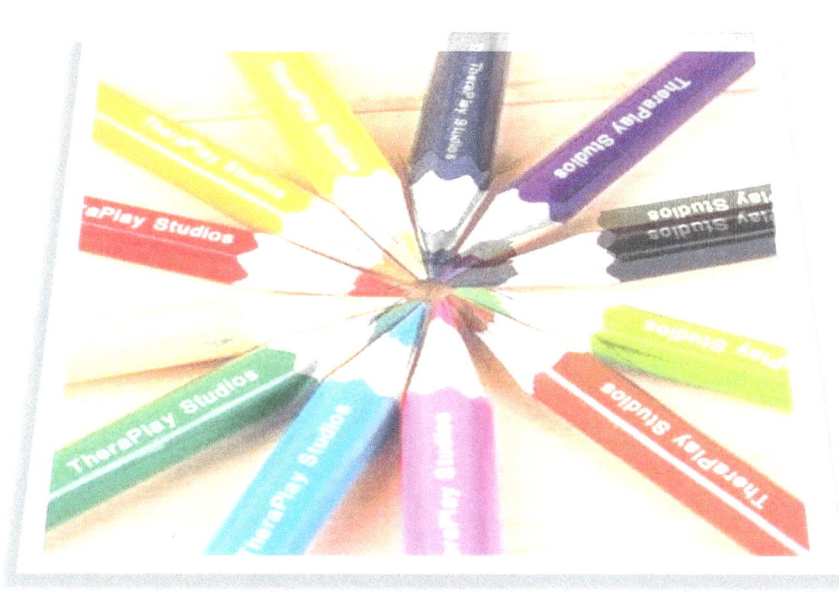

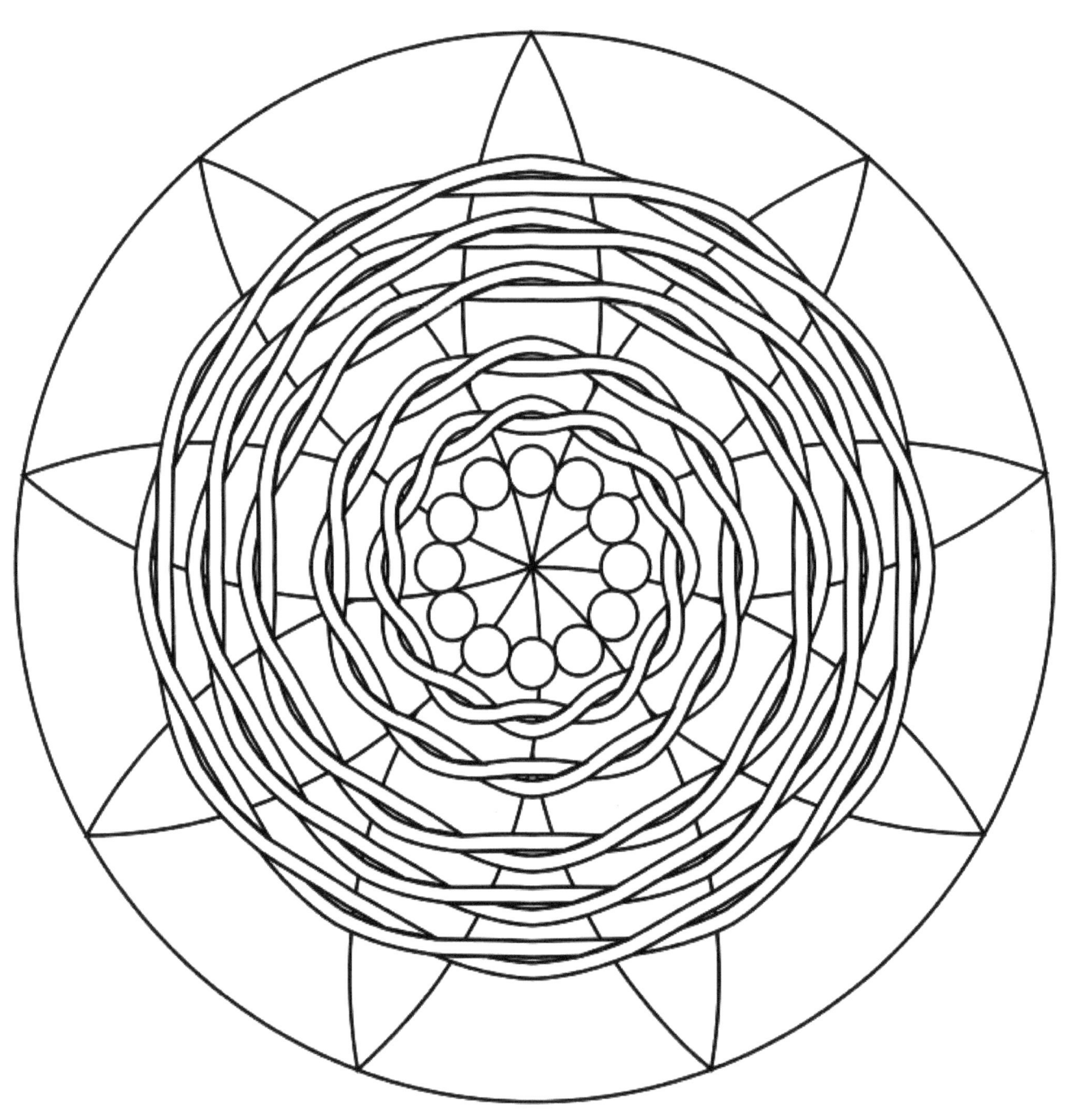

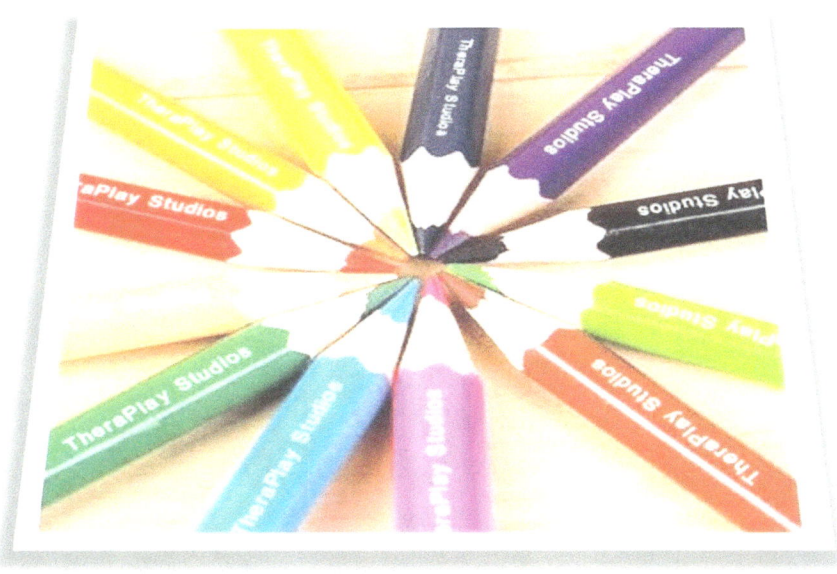

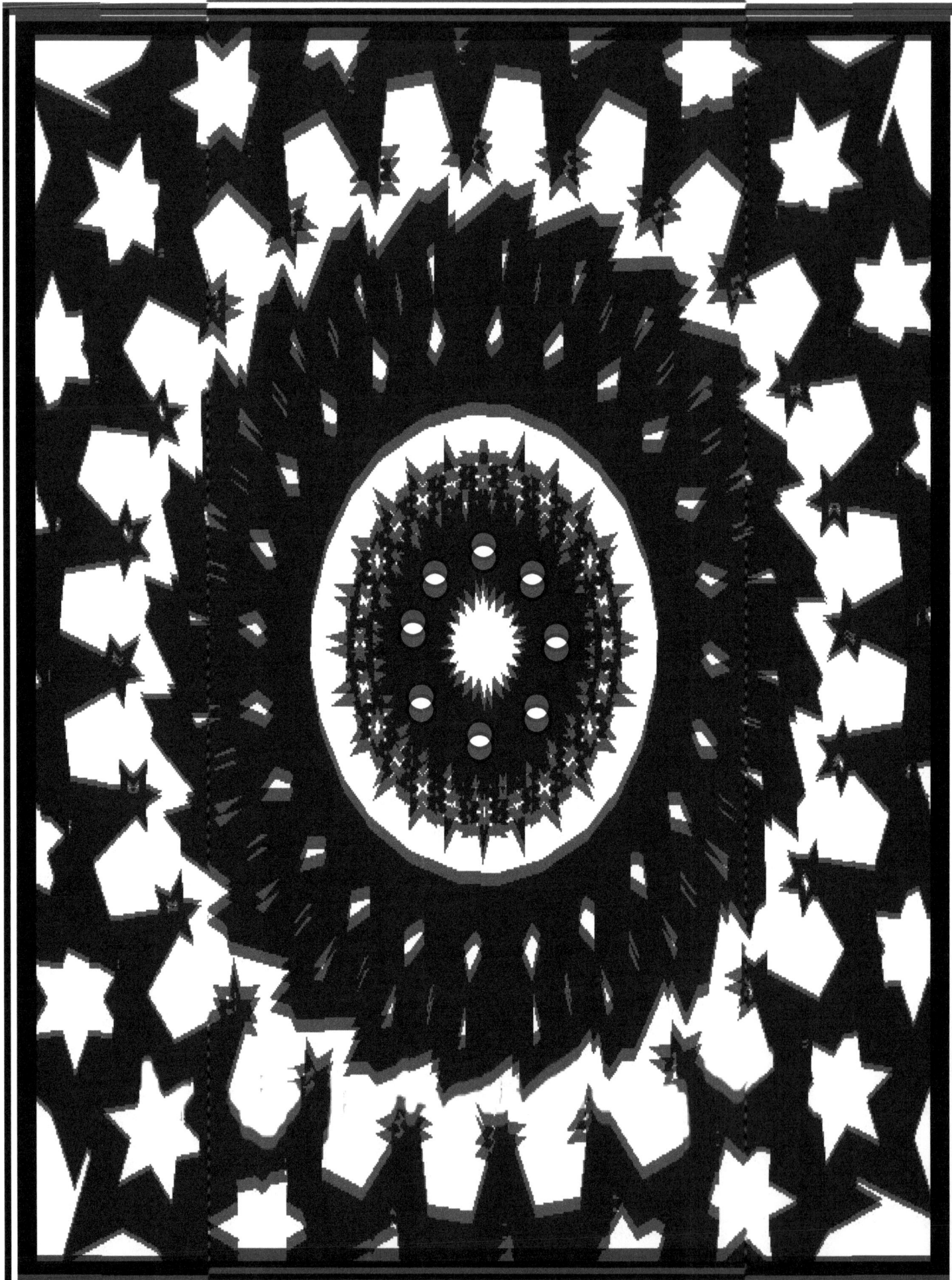

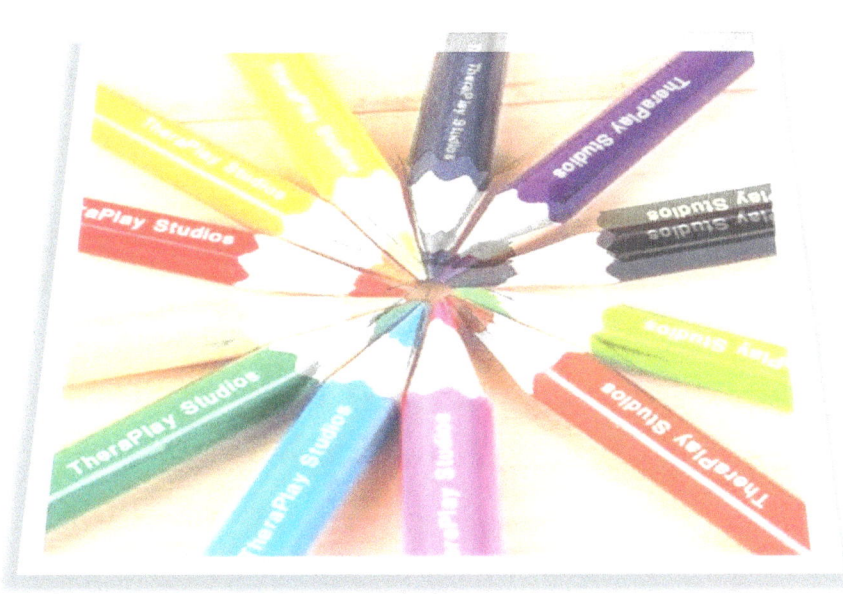

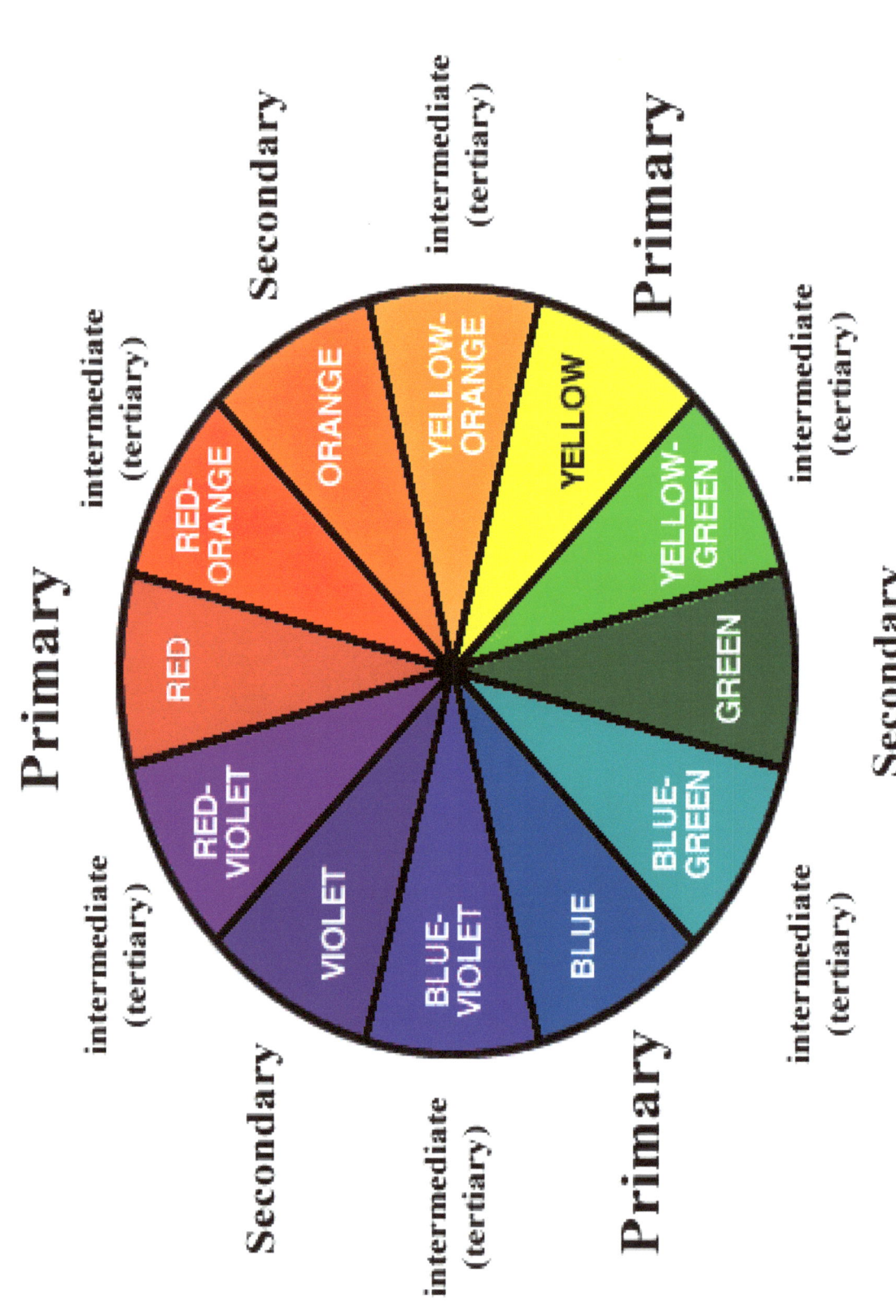

Find us on the web

www.arttheraplaystudios.com

@theraplaystudios

Facebook

Twitter

Instagram

www.ingramcontent.com/pod-product-compliance
Lightning Source LLC
Chambersburg PA
CBHW051951210526
45473CB00019B/1561